All rights reserved
Copyright © Crispin Emerson, 2022

The right of Crispin Emerson to be identified as the author of this
work has been asserted in accordance with Section 78
of the Copyright, Designs and Patents Act 1988

The book cover is copyright to Crispin Emerson

This book is published by
Grosvenor House Publishing Ltd
Link House
140 The Broadway, Tolworth, Surrey, KT6 7HT.
www.grosvenorhousepublishing.co.uk

This book is sold subject to the conditions that it shall not, by way of
trade or otherwise, be lent, resold, hired out or otherwise circulated
without the author's or publisher's prior consent in any form of binding or
cover other than that in which it is published and
without a similar condition including this condition being imposed
on the subsequent purchaser.

This book is a work of fiction. Any resemblance to
people or events, past or present, is purely coincidental.

A CIP record for this book
is available from the British Library

ISBN 978-1-80381-020-1

Poeticus Pictoralis II

Nautical & Natural

A small form of daffodil named "Poet's narcissi" and a style of painting that enhances the beauty of the subject

A second book of 60 natural, humorous and philosophical poems

By
Crispin

With original art from his family

Grosvenor House
Publishing Limited

Attributions

This is the second book in the Poeticus Pictoralis series;-

The 1st book was "Poeticus Pictoralis" by Crispin
This 2nd book is "Poeticus Pictoralis II Nautical & Natural" by Crispin

All the poems have been written by me

The original artwork is by my family;-

Mary's art are front & rear cover
and pages 3,7,11,13,15,17 & 29.
Angie's art are pages 33,35,67 & 89.
Jane's art are pages 37 & 96 and the 60 image.
Vic's art are pages 32 & 113.
Crispin's scribbles are pages 27,39,43,49,52,53, 61,63,73,75,77,79,91,97 & 99.

Dedications

This 2nd humble book of poetry is again dedicated with grateful thanks to:

My inspirational Mum (Mary), from whom I received my sensitivity to nature.

My sadly departed Dad (John), from whom I received the language and vocabulary to express my sensitivity.

My lovely kind-hearted wife (Angie).

My beautiful and talented daughters (Jane & Vic).

My friend, Mike and his family (including his Mum... Joy).

My friends & colleagues from the Bristol office (Karen, Annu, Anna).

To any of my customers, to whom I have read my poetry and who have expressed support and pleasure.

And finally the beautiful Dorset coastline and countryside that makes Bournemouth, Christchurch and Poole so wonderful...

Colourful Quotes

Plump sail... full like a big white pillow,
So firm and full, it had no chance to slacken or to billow,

I closed it quickly and understood, why its opening was slow,
I showed my palms to the one bar fire and in its orange glow,

In my weather-faded, baggy light green shorts,
I pushed my vessel through the shallow water... deep in thoughts,

Raucous crow grates his gravel voice in angry warning,
As the seagull comes too close, this cold, still, sunny morning,

And if for any reason you should fail to feed yourself,
There is no social worker, no seagull national health,

As I slightly sink, with gravity, my weight, by water halved,
The space between the rocks, is what the artist...nature carved,

Sea-birds fly head-on, into the wind,
Forward motion and the gusts...proportionately twinned,

The wind annuls the wails and cries of ocean gulls,
Suspended in their flight by gusts and lulls,

The giant hand, having roused the sea... points at land,
As if it were an enemy, with territory and ambition to expand,

About to rudely change its living state,
Later on, to grace, with parsley, my cracked old dinner plate,

The sea must have no memory, for it spills its edge again,
A drunken sailor is the sea... her land-legs are in vain,

My crusty eyes open slowly and flood my brain with light,
My face feels like a parchment, brittle leather pulled too tight,

I appreciate the lovely form,
Sanded by the water, sculpted by the storm,

Thin white masts of servant craft, gathered in a huddle,
Around the stick-like jetties, silver beams and planks, a muddle,

To squeal and run across the sand,
To dirty foot and dirty hand,

Scarlett buoys, like holly berries strewn,
Warn of where the man-made reef, was built and failed too soon,

Petulant and changeable... the wind embraces drama,
Sweeping mood-change influence, across this panorama,

Far away... small white cheeses, the pyramids of sails,
Mill around each other, with the breeze... exchanging hails,

The cubs, framed by the moonlight play, as silhouettes,
While captivated humans, hold their breath behind their nets,

My song like the laughter of all who come after,
In the form I possess…that's the black feathered dress,

Index of contents

Nautical   1-41

Natural   42-80

Of general interest   81-113

INDEX
Nautical poems

Green sea day	2
Cargo	4
Adam's day	8
Lake Road, Hamworthy	12
Seagull	14
The space in between	16
At Peveril point	18
Tableau	20
Roaring sea	22
Avon beach... Yesterday	23
Imagine	24
Fin	26
Crabbing at the quay	27
Little green motorboat	28
At sea	30
Brownsea Island from Shore Road in winter	33
My Utopia	34
Baiter point and Poole quay	36
Around Boscombe pier	38
Beach hut	40
Windy beach walk	41

Green sea day

What a day that was, the day we sailed to that deserted beach,
A green sea day, with white sea-spray, a day so out of reach…
Of an ordinary day… an extraordinary way… to travel,
The perfect way, to unknot a mind…simply to unravel,
As the dinghy pulls its way above the water… with the wind,
Plump sail… full like a big white pillow,
So firm and full, it had no chance to slacken or to billow,
But, pulled us like a magnet, to that sand-filled stretch of shore,
That island, always distant, on which I hadn't stood before,
A line of sea-borne detritus, showed where high-tide leaves this place,
Like a shady pencil moustache, on a shady salesman's face,

A tequila cocktail sea-sky, moved from peach to purple via pink,
I laughed, my comic mind had joked, "that's why it's called the drink",
Other sails were on the water... triangles in the distance,
My thoughts of leaving now, met with common-sense resistance,
We should wait until, the sky says, "we can go,"
And that is what we did... and then the wind did homeward blow.

Cargo

I took passage on a cargo ship, grey and black and smeared with rust,
Rectangular mountains of containers…Rows of mushroom rivets grey like dust,
My cabin small and practical, every space is used to give,
The tools of getting by each day, the devices, we use to live,

A sink, small like a pudding bowl, a single tap to fill it,
A kettle, if I want hot water…Cockroach! Slam! I kill it,
The bed is single and hangs by ropes suspended from the ceiling,
I pull a third rope, the bed folds in, a much more spacious feeling,

Bitter cold…Is what I feel, until I switch the fire on,
Walls, ceiling, floor and hull…all are made of iron,
Surround that with the icy sea and you create a fridge,
And I am still a lucky one, in my cabin below the bridge,

I paid extra for a porthole, roughly hub-cap sized,
Far above the waterline … my thought, as catch I prised,
It opened with a grudging stiffness, salt and water aged,
Whipping wind and spumy spray, past my port-hole raged,

I closed it quickly and understood, why its opening was slow,
I showed my palms to the one bar fire and in its orange glow,
I sat down and thought about, the reason I was there,
Making sure the legs were safely locked, on the folding patio chair,

I slept soundly on the simple bed, rocked naturally to sleep,
The movement of the cold dark sea, gave me a slumber deep,
I woke and went for breakfast, the canteen warm and bright,
A plate of beans and eggs and sausage, suited me just right,

Weeks had passed as into port, the giant ship was towed,
Ropes secured and gangplank lowered, I paid what I had owed,
I said farewell to sailors, those whom I had got to know,
With not a little sadness, did I let that big ship go,

I will always carry with me, the time I had for thought,
How wise it was of me that time, to travel from that port,
And not to rush the journey, by the taking of a plane,
For wisdom comes from time to think and wisdom keeps us sane.

Adam's day

I pumped and pumped until my Kayak, could inflate no more,
Lift it on my back and walk as turtle, to the line of shore,
In my weather-faded, baggy light green shorts,
I pushed my vessel through the shallow water... deep in thoughts,
I mounted up, with not a little wobbling,
Laughter from two gulls nearby...or maybe they were squabbling,
I raised my paddle and plunged it down and back,
The craft moved swiftly forward in response to the attack,
Weaving through the moorings of the idle unused boats,
Tethered to the bulbous plastic brightly-coloured floats,
I waited 'til I reached the open water of the bay,
To drop the nylon line, with spinning lure, I hoped would pay,
With a fish or two...a Gurnard or a Mack,
Yes...a Mackerel would indeed, make a lovely mid-day snack,

I leave the line to animate in the wake of my canoe,
And paddle to increase the size…of the island in my view,
Half an hour of water lapping fast on either side,
And my feet are on the island sand, on which only I reside,
I take my rod from the rubber canvas crease which held it tight,
Turn the handle on the reel. There's resistance… good…it might,
Mean a fish has joined the party, not happy to attend.
My hopes are further bolstered as I see the thin rod bend,
Coming through the shallow water, my lunch… unwilling…dragged,
Unhooked…I hit him with a priest…no service… his body is bagged,
In the lee of a sandy grass-topped scoop of man-high cliff,
I make a ring of rocks. Time has frozen…it's as if,

I am making fire, like man has always done,
I am making fire and feeling like I am the only one,
Who's smart enough to catch and cook a fish.
Well...smarter than those, who at this moment, could but only wish,
To be where I am...and not where they are now.
Working in an office, seeking when, who, where and how...
My fish is ready...I see the steam escaping from the foil,
I had cleaned it. Lemon slices and I drizzled olive oil,
The soft hot flesh fell easily off the bone,
As I ate...I was happy that, I was here... and all alone,
With one exception...A seagull stood and looked,
At the fish he thinks I stole from him...and sacrilege...I cooked.

Lake Road, Hamworthy

Lake Road ends and joins the seashore,
A little piece of land fulfils the role, Cars and road…no more,
A bridge between the states, upturned boats in dis-repair,
One such boat has formed a pond…no holes there,
But others show the signs of being dumped,
No longer to the water humped,
With grunts and heaves to move the watercraft,
To where it moves with nature…its future is to aft,
Shattered now and holed below the line,
Dull and soiled, abandoned to the brine,

Raucous crow grates his gravel voice in angry warning,
As the seagull comes too close, this cold, still, sunny morning,
Abandoned buoys, chained to sandy bed,
Whilst swelling clouds of cotton wool, loiter overhead,

Rugged crumbling slipway...gently lapped,
As beak containing winkle shell is less than
    gently tapped,
Hard against the stony concrete wedge,
The breaking of the shell, at water's edge,
Leaving shattered fragments littering the
    shore,
Just like the fragments of the boats, that will
    be used no more.

Seagull

Seagull...why do you wail?
You wheel and turn as though you are,
   a wind-inflated sail,
As pure a white as ever could be seen,
In contrast to the pale thin sky and freezing
   sea of green,

Seagull...what do you mean?
Are you telling of your sadness, of brutal
   nature seen?
Your cry can pierce the silence in the air,
Even though the wind is booming, thudding...
   crashing through my hair,

Seagull...you have no other choice,
But to fly and fish, defend your catch, use your
   screeching voice,
To warn the other seagulls, who have no
   option... but to try...
To steal the silver from your grasp, before your
   chance to fly,

Seagull...Is it true you have no friend?
Do the means of how you stay alive, justify the
   end?
Selfish for the shellfish and elbowed to the
   front,
Is this the limit of your needs? Fish and chips
   are all you want?

Seagull…I know it couldn't be harder,
You must eat **now**. There is no store, no refrigerated larder,
And if for any reason you should fail to feed yourself,
There is no social worker, no seagull national health,

Seagull…You must be the bird you are… as made,
You must scream at other seagulls, their space you must invade,
Rip the wriggling fish from another seagull's beak,
Be the strong one at all times, for death awaits the weak.

The space in between

The point at which the precious land, meets the perilous sea,
Is the point at which I feel as though, my spirit may float free…
There's something about the wild, untameable waves,
And how the saline water, breaking on the shore, behaves,
The rockets of foamy spume ricochet upward to the sky,
To fall in hopeless failure, the escape is thwarted by…
Gravity…another law of nature takes effect,
The spray returns to the sea…unable to defect,
A rock that has no mystery above, the slurping water slapping,
Below the spotlight, is unknown, below the furious clapping,
A home maybe for creatures, hiding in their fear,
Communal memory…distant thoughts of those that disappear,
Bonds we do not understand, those creatures form,
As human, it is hard to fathom, things beyond our norm,

The yellow sand like syrup runs between the random rocks,
Pleasure is the feel of naked foot...discarded socks,
As I slightly sink, with gravity, my weight, by water halved,
The space between the rocks, is what the artist...nature carved,
Often it's the space between, that carries greater meaning,
Just as this life, may well be, the space that's intervening,
Between two others of description... as yet unknown,
But, surely the space that's in between, is a space in which...we've grown.

At Peveril Point

To the north…faint Miami skyline of
 Bournemouth in the distance,
My eyes, behind my glasses, water with the
 wind's persistence,
Ruler-straight, the rocky runways assailed by
 relentless waves,
Affecting only locally, how the sea behaves,

From the point at Peveril, you can see,
How different…in one single place, the sea can
 actually be,
For where it's sheltered from the wind…it's soft
 and slow and calm,
Yet…fifty yards to the south, the bitter waves,
 would do you harm,

Sea-birds fly head-on, into the wind,
Forward motion and the gusts…proportionately
 twinned,
The net result? They hover…beak and eyes
 pointing south,
Looking for the fish they'll pluck, from sea with
 bony mouth,

Two times triple aspect glazed, the watch-tower
 ever scans,
The vicious seas, for unfortunate sailors…
 undergoing a change of plans,

"Old Harry" juts out to the north,
Smugglers in the past came forth,
To test the strength of the local constabulary,
Rum and "Backy" hauled ashore, with colourful Dorset vocabulary,

Round the head, into the harbour's arms,
The old coastguard's cottages...rustic treasures...charms,
Exude from every ancient stone and rock,
Used by Georgian fisherman to build this lovely block,
Of homes, for those indebted to the sea,
Blessed are those, who live there now,
Who look...and love...and be.

Tableau

Place your tartan cushion, upon that flat rock there,
A boulder sits behind you, keeps the wind out of your hair,
The violent breaking of the waves upon the rocks below,
Casts sparkling beads of rainbow seeds, a Vegas fountain show,

The wind annuls the wails and cries of ocean gulls,
Suspended in their flight by gusts and lulls,
White and grey against the clouds of white and grey this day,
Refusing to be beaten down until they've had their say,

The ragged creases of the rolling fabric of the sea,
Appear to give a solid surface, bark around a tree,
Imperfections, texture changes, anomalies abound,
All of nature's hallmarks, even when you're not around,

You see the burly clouds let a shard of sun escape,
A lime-light beam, highlights a scene, a wave with golden drape,
All the sea around it, bows and steps back to defer,
Respecting as they do, the part the sun chose to prefer,

Keep this painting in your mind… keep its rolling motion,
Remember the cold grey rocks below and the freezing green glass ocean,
Don't forget the absent sun, breaking through the ceiling,
Carry nature's glories in you…feel what nature's feeling.

Roaring sea

The wild sea roars with riotous applause,
As it rolls and breaks upon our island shores,
Cold white foam is whipped into suds,
Showing the wind's direction, as it scuds…
Along the hardened sandy line at water's edge,
Draped with jade green weed… Neptune's veg,

Out beyond… the wave's response, to the centrifuge,
To spinning earth and pulling moon… is huge,
The Gods have dropped a mighty rock,
Into the ocean… the waves… a reaction to the shock,
The giant hand, having roused the sea… points at land,
As if it were an enemy, with territory and ambition to expand,
Full of fabulous fury, the cavalry of waves… Mount their siege,
To founder like a gentleman… Noblesse Oblige,
Their final act, as energy is spent,
To ensure the raucous air is rent…
With noise to justify their power,
Then trickle back… for the body of the Sea to then devour.

Avon beach...yesterday

Yesterday, I went to Avon beach...took my Mum along,
It's winter/spring, so the sea was out of reach... seagull's song,
Greeted us, alighting from the car,
The needles off the Isle of Wight, misty... near... not far,
Mum was there to scratch-sketch random shapes,
Trapping skeletons of biro lines, before the form escapes,
I was there to translate into word,
The feelings of the smells and sights and sounds that could be heard,
We made a slightly awkward-looking pair,
Dashing on our notepads...some wondering why we're there,
But awkward is not remotely how we feel,
As we are only capturing, what we all know, to be real,
The beauty, of the nature, of our county,
The land and sand that meets the sea and all its glorious bounty...

Imagine

Close your eyes and let your mind float light…
and gently land,
Upon the sun-warmed rainbow-glinting,
powdered golden sand,
All concerns and cares are left behind…
Leave your body…this adventure, only needs
your mind,
Every step brings comfort to the soles, of
softened feet,
Everywhere you rest your gaze, is natural and
complete,
It's warm, but cooling breezes lightly stroke
your lovely hair,
Your oiled skin is tanning well and smooth
beyond compare.

The clear blue sea spills its edge, over custard
sand,
Sees its error and retracts, with apologies to
land,
The sea must have no memory, for it spills its
edge again,
A drunken sailor is the sea… her land-legs are
in vain,
The moon though hiding out of human sight,
Drags the sea across the surface, everyday…
and night.

You walk along the boundary of the sea,
And nowhere in your body-mind is pain allowed to be,
You climb up to a crop of smooth warmed rock,
Graphite-grey in colour...you sit...your eyes take stock,
Search the still quiet underwater nooks,
Of salty pools where tiny fearsome creatures... exchanging looks,
Ready minute weapons, of defence,
Though generally in nature, they all have much more sense,
Than to court a confrontation without the need,
As all they really have to do, is eat and grow and breed,
See that pinkie-whitey-silver jewel brightly shine?
Mother of the pearl, which went to school within the brine,
Nature showing us a mother's pride,
And we with all our riches...toss this masterpiece aside?

It's time now that you floated slowly back,
To where you left your body and the time that you must track,
Before you start to list all of the things you have to do,
Remember how important is... the floating of the you.

FIN

I'm looking at the very tip of the rod that I have planted,
Cork handle sits in the venting hole, the rod itself is slanted,
Angled (no pun intended), like an old red clay tiled roof,
The insistent jerking of that tip… all I'll have as proof,
That away in the cold and mysterious dim-lit undersea,
A silver muscle, scaled with probing snatching mouth may be,
About to rudely change its living state,
Later on, to grace, with parsley, my cracked old dinner plate,
A comb of bones and head and tail, I'll scrape into the waste,
His final act…repeating… his distinctive fishy taste… fishy taste…

FIN.

Crabbing at the quay

Mudeford quay…when sun is beaming,
Families, laughing, squealing, teaming…
Up to catch the greatest number…
Of dopey crabs, from their slumber,
By bacon with the hidden hook,
Just a nibble, just a look,
Yanked from seabed, to excited laughter,
Pulled off hook, in bucket after,
There to share a shameful cell,
With other dopey crabs as well,
Until the folks have had enough…
Of hand-line catching Crabby stuff,
A count ensues amongst the fishers,
Craning heads from well-wishers,
Five for the little boy, in the jeans,
Eight for big sister, in her teens,
Mum and Dad had caught some too,
They didn't count them…well, would you?
Buckets tipped, Crustacea returned,
Family pub lunch had been earned,
The Crabs went back to eat more bacon,
Another family's bait is taken…

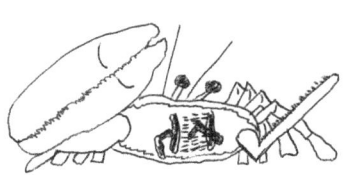

Little green motor-boat

Shells and shale are crunching beneath my feet,
As I take my steps towards the little motor boat, so sweet,
Beach-hut green… the little hull is painted,
The air with scent of seaweed and seagull drops is tainted,
The little boat bobs, like tail is wagging,
The tether to the buoy which holds him there… is slightly sagging,
As if the little boat has come to greet me,
Excited… as am I, to get out upon the sea,
The sky, though heavy, with some murk within the cloud,
Encourages me to make an old-time statement… said out loud,
"There is enough blue, to make a pair of Sailor's trousers,"
My grandma used to say it, as she dried her flowery blouses,
On the line, that stretched from house to garden's end,
The blue in sky the measure, upon which the drying would depend,
She also used to say it, to her regular paying-guests,
So that they would go out for the day and not be household pests,
Well…I for one, will not be stuck inside,
On a day when I can be afloat and upon the waves I'll ride,

I walk around the upturned rowing boat,
Turtle-like they leave it, when it's not afloat,
My feet, shod in flip flops, get wet as I climb aboard,
The little green motor-boat, now adrift... now un-moored,
Fires into life... I've pulled the string,
Which makes this little character... a living breathing thing,
We slowly make our way, away from shore,
To the place of singularity... the place that we adore...

At sea

The giant seabird circles high and he...sees all around,
He notes a tiny wooden speck...seas all around,
Tilting wings forward down, he swoops in close to see,
If edible to seagull taste, a morsel may there be,

My crusty eyes open slowly and flood my brain with light,
My face feels like a parchment, brittle leather pulled too tight,
Where am I? I don't remember how I ended here,
I don't remember anything...I'm acquainted now with fear,

No knowledge is there in my mind of who I may have been,
No memory of my character or faces I have seen,
I'm lying on my back and looking up into the sky,
In a little clinker rowing boat...I have no idea... why?

I still don't move…I listen as the water slurps and slaps,
The starboard side of the boat, where the planks are ridged in laps,
Starboard…that's a seaman's term. Maybe I'm a sailor?
Looking now at the rags I'm in…unlikely I'm a tailor,

An enormous seagull gently lands and sits and bobs off port,
My second nautical reference…"I'm a sailor!" I retort,
The seagull seems to nod as if he should know a Jack,
I also fear that he may know…this tar won't make it back,

I look around inside the boat for any sign of water,
Nothing there…only proof…my suffering will be shorter,
I could try and catch the seagull, drink his blood and eat his meat,
Use the feathers to make a screen…protect me from the heat,

Distaste at killing filled my mind…this at least I gleaned,
Unlikely I'm a murderer…I'm good…I'm not a fiend,
How fate put me here to die, forgotten and alone,
I think I'm destined not to know…and then I hear… a mobile phone.

Brownsea Island from Shore road in winter

Tumbled reeds of straw…a politician's wig,
Leads to sandy waterline where Oyster-catchers dig,
With scimitar beaks of coral ivory, split to form a tool,
Sea-food is so plentiful, within this bay in Poole,
Thin white masts of servant craft, gathered in a huddle,
Around the stick-like jetties, silver beams and planks, a muddle,
A low brown smear of textured mat…In winter Brownsea looks like that,
Hunkered down twixt sky and sea…Brownsea squats there patiently,
Flags protest and struggle, attempting flight,
Flapping on the tether on the pole, that holds them tight,
They wish to cease their advertising role,
And soar into the air, at last… as if they have a soul.

My Utopia

A winding yellow path… of imbedded sandy gravel,
Provides a way from "Hillside house," for feet and paws to travel,
The languid one-mile walk, through grassy glades, with trees,
But, never losing sight ahead, of the warm blue aqua seas,
I wear linen… it's white and light and breathes,
My shirt, is cotton, white and collared… but no sleeves,
A loosely tailored jacket… trousers baggy…yet somehow smart,
Chestnut-coloured sandals help me, to feel the part,
The part is free of worry and concerns,
Everyone is happy and no racist insult burns,
All of the souls, that I could ever meet,
Are pleased to see me and never fail to greet,
My arrival as a positive event,
And I…in turn am happy, for Utopia, will not relent,
The widening path opens its arms, as if to say,
"This is where I led you…now you must choose your way,"
The sea in front, the beach to left and right,
I stand and watch the seagulls, as they hover in their flight,
I turn and look back up the hill, to home,
"Like a cricket pavilion." I say to myself, as the beach, I start to comb,

I find only natural things, washed up upon the shore,
A piece of silver driftwood… a tree it was before,
It lived and died and fell into the sea,
For time and tide, to craft it and present its art to me,
I appreciate the lovely form,
Sanded by the water, sculpted by the storm,
It will have a new life, leant against the wall,
In the pavilion on the hillside, by the coat-rack in the hall.

Baiter Point and Poole quay

The sea was very still today, at Baiter, near the quay,
The sun laid light upon it, in a shimmering silver vee,
Patient silhouettes... the hulks of hulls, float and wait,
For the unexpected visit of their human owner-mate,
Far away... small white cheeses, the pyramids of sails,
Mill around each other, with the breeze... exchanging hails,
The marina stacked with costly pleasure craft,
With canted, sloping, angled rears, Sailors call the aft,
Seagulls, Sparrows, Starlings... gathered by the chip shop,
As people cast their crumbs, to see the flap and peck and hop,
Further up the quay...
Walk and you could see...
A Seagull (roughly chicken-sized), stabs a slab of butchered Plaice,
Unable to make it small enough, to shove into his beaky face,
Yards away a smaller seabird floats like rubber duck,
Waiting for the tide to change and with it change his luck,
A limping Pidgeon with ugly mangled toe,
Survives okay round here...lots of food you know,

Across the water at the dock, a giant ship,
Opens up its deck-doors, for the cranes to lucky-dip,
And pull the cargo from its cavernous tum,
The crew are gathered on the bridge, for pay and tots of rum,
The sea was very still today, at Baiter, near the quay,
But life is never still you know… nor should it ever be.

Around Boscombe Pier

A sunny day came our way, this March-month's trailing end,
I'd called round, poems to sound and with Mum some hours spend,
On Sea road hill, I parked the car, Boscombe pier…not too far,
We sauntered down towards the sea…mother and son…Mum & me…

Concrete car park legs…hold the boarded walk above the waves,
In the lifeguard's hut binoculars scan, to anticipate the saves,
That may arise from the water-loving hoards,
Some of whom are standing as they paddle on their boards,
Scarlett buoys, like holly berries strewn,
Warn of where the man-made reef, was built and failed too soon,
Horizon haunted by the ghosts of cruises not now taken,
Luxury travel "Floatels" lying empty and forsaken,

On the prom, the primary colours of felt-roofed, saw-toothed huts,
Day-time houses, rolled up "trousis," sinking crazy putts,
Concrete rocks are playground blocks, delighting all the young,
Pandemic Covid will abate, Boscombe will again inflate, once more a healthy lung.

Beach hut

Beach hut on the promenade,
Brightly coloured planked façade,
Drop the drawbridge, open doors,
Fruit drinks sucked through shiny straws,
Radio plays "Beach boys" tunes,
Sculpted sand and shifting dunes,
Many Junes spent here in rapture,
Cell phones only used to capture,
Moments frozen in the sun,
Special moments having fun,
Beach hut puts us in the now,
Help for those, who've forgotten how,
To squeal and run across the sand,
To dirty foot and dirty hand,
To splash… and care not where time goes,
To towel out sand, from between their toes,
Beach hut, painted vivid red,
You're more than just a seafront shed…

Windy beach walk

The strong and steady metronomic beat,
Of waves on shore… my heart and marching feet,
The promenade provides the vast flat stage,
On which I walk and feel the warm wind rage,
Which cries and with crescendo of percussion,
Holds me up, then stops abruptly… ending the discussion,
My eyes and mouth, assailed by flying sand,
Whipped up upon the wind, my face slapped by its hand,
I spit, the single grains and put my finger in my eye,
Scraping tender eyeball, as abrasive pushes by,
Petulant and changeable… the wind embraces drama,
Sweeping mood-change influence, across this panorama,
When it's in my face, the wind is akin to foe,
Changes tack, when I turn my back, it pushes me to go,
Reluctantly, I take the door I'm shown,
And exit as requested… all resistance… blown.

Index

Natural poems

Morning	43
Urban Fox	44
Blackbird	46
The test	47
Brush stroke	48
In**duck**tion	50
Heron	52
It's living	53
The greater nature	54
Pigeon	56
Summer rain	57
Sat in the park	58
Lonely Spider	60
Hydrangea echoes	61
The beautiful pink rose	62
Butterflies and Bees	63
When I get my orchard	64
The river Stour near Iford	66
The view from 'garden end'	68
Dorset man	70
Hip upon the briar	72
The Oak is dead	74
Dead Mouse	75
Hedgehog hotel	76
Sweet the Robin	78
The tree by the fence	79
I will be a bird	80

Morning

How sweet is the morning and its timely
   arrival?
How fresh is the air through the windows flung
   wide?
The night has prepared for the daily revival,
Nowhere for darkness and silence to hide,

The bushes and branches a stage for the
   singers,
Their whole tiny bodies force notes from their
   beaks,
A fanfare of greeting, the little joy-bringers,
This is the morning…hear how it speaks.

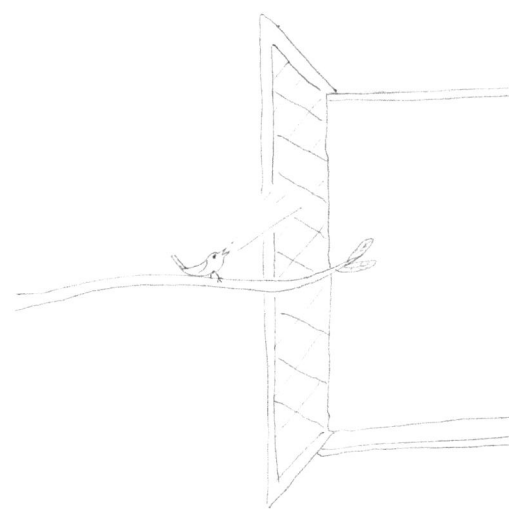

Urban fox

Hello Fox…We made each other jump!
I was going to the food bin, these scraps and peels to dump,
Your almond-shaped, hazel-coloured eyes,
Opened wider quickly, at the instant of surprise,
But, fear is all I saw…no malice showing,
You pause, a quick assessment. Are you staying? Are you going?
You wait…I sense you've seen the bag I hold,
How is it, you've got so brave? Grown to be so bold?
This town was built on fields you would have roamed,
So many human families, this new estate has homed,
Your ginger fur, is orange like the brick,
Co-incidental camouflage, nature's cunning trick,
An urban fox, the smartest of your breed,
Originally from the woodland, you've come to town to feed,
The cubs, framed by the moonlight play, as silhouettes,
While captivated humans, hold their breath behind their nets,

In darkness from their bedroom, the predator observes,
The natural entertainment, your fox cub family serves,
With practiced disappointment, you turn your fiery face,
And pad away so silently, to a more productive place.

Blackbird

Of what do I sing as the morning rises and as
   the night is falling?
I sing with the knowledge, that music like mine
   is my right, as it is my calling,
I sing with glorious ease, of the towering trees,
I sing of food to be found in the soft earthy
   ground,
My song like the laughter of all who come after,
In the form I possess...that's the black
   feathered dress,
With the beak of orange to yellow...I'm a
   blackbird...I'm a fellow,
The morning can't resist, the prospect of being
   kissed,
By the intricate notes, I've projected... it floats,
Musically and magically on the morning mist...
   the lyrical twist.

I punctuate the close of day to tell,
The interval of night shall pass and in the
   morning...I will mark it well.

The test

Great winds have come to test the nest,
Of all that fly on feather and wing,
And punish those, who chose to rest,
And did too little…
Who used the dry twig, lighter…but brittle,
Whose eggs will fly before they're hatched…
Because the nest…too light…detached,
And sailed on winds of uncanny power,
Cut down too soon…vase and flower,
Those winds are meant only for seagulls,
Or hawks, falcons, powerful eagles,
Not for birds of minimal stature,
Only for flyers who are, animal catcher,
The eggs, if unbroken,
Will be sucked by a fox, rudely awoken,
By the gale…his fur roughly-whipping,
His mouth…gently sipping,
With ghastly politeness,
The nest…with its lightness,
Has blown all away…the evidence,
Like its occupants…no longer in residence.

Brush stroke

The low grass verge was spotted with the yellow sneeze,
Of Dandy-lion heads, growing as they please,
Then a bank of bluebells…a purple sheen,
Combined in suffragette colours, lovely to be seen,
The mauve appears to hover, as though a mist of wonder,
Has risen from the fertile soil, that forms when leaves go under,
Further back beyond the bluebell's magic haze,
I see a shock of vibrant yellow…a flowering field of maize,
I'm rocked by the combination of the purple…yellow…green,
A sandwich of the brightest colours, I have ever seen,
A geologist's precious sample of layered rock,
Would pale by comparison… become a dull and worthless block,
The artist of the universe, had run the mighty brush,
Across the landscape canvas, in an horizontal rush,
The casual nature of the master-stroke,
Belies fantastic detail… lying under nature's cloak.

In**duck**tion

The mother duck was moving slowly... and keeping low,
Her chest and tummy sliding through the grass... she mustn't show,
The circling buzzards patrolling the skies above,
Her fluffy young entourage, gathered in the shelter of her love,
Her little paddle feet, could not be seen... she seemed to slide,
A small brown smudge, attempting to cross to the other side,
Of the fairway, from the rough, to the sanctuary of the pond,
Where the reeds and rushes fortify with sharp, offensive frond,
Enough for a mum, her floating family to hide,
If only she could get them home, from the other side,
The little flock of downy, brownie charges huddled tight,
Glued...a single entity...attached to mum, by fright,
They copied Mother's movement, learning as they went,
With total concentration, survival... their intent,

She reached the fairway, where the grass is short,
Now she was a sprinter…survival…is the sport,
She stood full height…all secrecy she shed,
She ran as fast as possible…she had to, or they were dead,
The brown smudge seemed to float across the grass,
Thirty seconds… seems like hours, when you pray the danger will pass,
But pass, it did…for now at least they're saved,
And the chicks had learned a lot from the way that mum behaved,
Enough, one hopes … that they will have their life,
And live to be a mother, or a husband, or a wife.

Heron

I watched you wading in the shallow stream,
Not so shallow really...that's just how, you made it seem,
Your legs are long, to help you with that task,
What size would be your Salopettes? I really shouldn't ask,
Your eye is very serious and sharp,
As you scan the moving water for an unsuspecting carp,
Your beak is like a fencer's jabbing foil,
Waiting for the moment, when unleashed by neck's uncoil,
If you fly...and fly you sometimes do,
Those useful legs, soon become, an encumbrance to you,
So you let them dangle down, as your wings wave slow goodbye,
Elegance personified...to this admiring eye.

It's living

The stone that circles the trunk of the oak,
Is lifting…
An arboreal effort to stave off the choke,
Is fitting…
I don't want its surrender,
I have sylvan feelings most tender,
It's growing…
I actually like the look of the stone,
As it shifts to the vertical from the prone,
It's natural…
So, I'll let the stone lift around the tree,
Because, after all, it's bigger than me,
It's living…

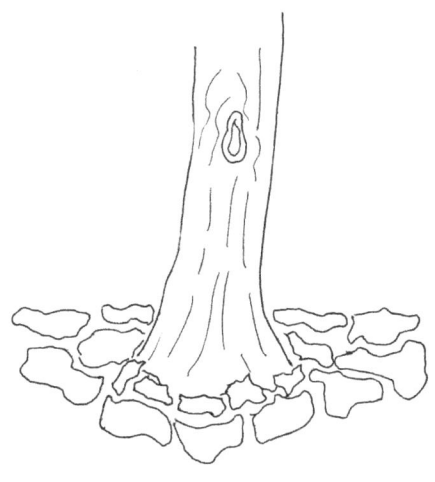

The Greater nature

Walk for 30 minutes through the columns of the trees,
Until the traffic's hum, no longer carries on the breeze,
And sit upon that stump there… the tree has now departed,
The trunk was felled and sawn, then to the world of men was carted,
Look around… and hear the music of the birds,
Focus on the notes and soon you'll get the words,
Experience and maturity tunefully displayed,
An advert for the singer, about good decisions made,
Hoping to seduce a feathery mate,
And add some new arias, to his song, so consummate,
Wet and waxy beech leaves, cloak the path in nutty brown,
Holding precious moisture, even though they have come down,
Saving bugs and crawling things from drying in the sun,
Vital cogs in eco-wheels, for food and deeds they've done,

Down the hill you walk, the trees still perpendicular,
Midges fly in mouth and eye, going nowhere in particular,
You see ferns of exotic construction,
They hide and thrive in shade… a logical deduction,
At the bottom of the hill, a trickling stream,
Cold, brackish water, with unseen lives it will teem,
For in the greater nature, than the nature we can see,
All the reasons for everything, must surely somewhere be?
But… for a moment of unrecorded length,
You are free to charge your core, of nature-loving strength,
And be at peace with the world, walking in the wood,
And feel the health and well-being… and know it's done you good.

Pigeon

Plump, grey, round when on the ground...you appear to me,
The same as when you sit upon, a branch high in the tree,
Oh... but when you fly, you give the lie, to round and portly form,
Scorching sprint or marathon...both you can perform,
The speed with which you fly from lazy place to lazy place,
Would shame the busy robin...would bring redness to his face,
For in the realm of sovereign sky, you have urgency unmatched,
By any other creature ... (Save the raptors)... ever hatched.

Summer rain

Rain can still fall in summer, around the end of June,
It reminds us, that the other seasons, will be calling soon,
Summer rain… an interruption by a friend,
To the lover… with whom we wish our summertime to spend,
For rain in summer curtails us… and always will,
But, optimistic souls will see, the birdbath slowly fill,
As the lawn and flowers, gratefully receive,
The tear-tracks on the dusty leaf…deceive,
Summer rain… vital to the growth and health of things,
And the blackbird and the robin, wash beneath their wings.

Sat in the park

Today, I sat on the grass in the park…still and like a tree I became,
Losing thoughts of identity, passwords and even my name,
Outward went my senses like branch and root,
And inward came reward, as if it were…long-forgotten fruit,
What did I hear and smell and sense?
Things that I could never feel when life is so intense,
The creaking timber of heavy bough, forced by breeze to dip,
The noise that Nelson's sailors heard at night upon their ship?
The song of Robin, both shrill and soft in equal portion,
The soft to woo a lover, the shrill a rival's caution,
The breeze has no sound, but that which resistance will endow,
The cup (my ear) hears rustling and rushing and sudden silence now,
Chlorophyll from the shortened grass, upon which I sit,
Assails my nose, it happens I suppose…when people are mowing it,

The yellow-faded straw of the separated strands,
Dry out and will be blown away to unknown foreign lands,
A tiny, shiny stumbling beetle climbs over blades of grass,
To us…a surface flat…is to him a great morass,
These labours of survival and of lives lived in the rough…
…Are visible to all of us…if we just stay quiet enough.

Lonely Spider

The webs of lonely Spiders... scary,
Suspended nets for catching the tiny and
   unwary...
Flying suckers of the air,
Who go from flower to flower, as if they have
   no care,
The lonely Spider waits...
If company arrives, she celebrates,
She'll wrap a present and be excited,
Even though the guest, had never been invited,
She will drink the health of any,
Of the visitors... and there are many,
Butterflies and Bees,
Grasshoppers, with bony knees,
Moths and tiny little flies,
But, still she doesn't realise,
She will always be a lonely Spider,
With only memories of her guests... inside her...

Hydrangea echoes

Keep the Hydrangea watered, when the sun is casting heat,
Or else you'll see the branches sag, the leaves down at your feet,
The lacy caps, with shrivelled petals clad,
Turn to crisps of flavour… you'll have never had,
No! De-hydrangea, is not to be allowed,
Keep the Hydrangea watered…bushy, upright, proud,
And you will be rewarded, as amongst the green leaves crowd,
Pompom heads of multi-petalled glory,
Colours subtle blues and pinks… hinting at a bygone story,
When those who lived, lived in the shadow of war,
Determined to keep the sunlight shining, as it was before,
The round and flowery heads… typify the staunch resilience,
Of a generation, strong in mind… and admirable in their brilliance.

The beautiful pink rose

See the beautiful rose,
It gives the senses pleasure…the eyes, the nose,
Petals pink…like the softest skin,
Attract me closer, it draws me in,
Then the scent… a hint of treasure,
Too sweet to explain or ever hope to measure,
A pollinator smaller must be found,
Unless of course, I put my nose in, all that is around,
Then I have been busy, like a bee,
Far too busy to have had the time to see,
The many minarets of buds… thrusting,
Above the open flower heads… trusting,
That they will get their chance to open out,
To replace the dissolving has-beens and to shout,
"Look at me! I am the beauty of the now,"
"And you must love me always, in any way… you know how."

Butterflies and Bees

Butterflies and Bees,
All are well disposed towards these,
The butterfly with canvas-painted wing,
Whose mazy flight... an unpredicted thing,
Stuttering and quickly changing course,
At the whim of nature's wind-blown force,
A sudden gust could take him there,
Or here's as good... as anywhere,
Uncurls his rolled up tongue,
For nectar sweet, as any song that's sung,
He rolls it back, a paper party-whistle,
Sat upon the flower-head, of an heavily armoured thistle,
His friend the bee, like lunar-module landing,
Comes to join him... they have an understanding,
Neither will do harm to careless folk,
Who are oblivious to nature... that's their nature... that's the joke...

When I get my orchard…

An acre of land, I will plant by my hand and happy to dirty be,
The air is rent, with almond-scent and sweet-fruit generosity,
I'll randomly plant the pink-blossomed cherry,
And arranged round the base of the trunk, there'll be very…
Beautiful wild flowers, which in turn will attract…
Lacewings and Ladybirds to feast on the aphids, which would have attacked…
The plump dark red cherries, ever so sweet,
Which melt in the mouth like an Eden-found treat,
With cherries go pears (Doyenne du Comice) sweet and soft,
I see the whole picture, sitting as I am, framed by the hatch of the loft,
Of the upstairs of the storage shed, where I dangle my legs,
And listen to the clicking sound, as the wheel blows around and the pegs…
Hold the cards to the spokes and scare some birds away,
At least, when the wind blows in the cooler part of autumn's day,

Bees will reside in the hives…I'll provide,
Coming and going…no hint of pesticide,
Will be allowed in my orchard, which I will happily share,
With most of the creatures who wish to be there,
An embarrassment of plums which borders on fury,
As red turns to purple, I'll be cleared by the jury…
For by… giving so many away,
I will mitigate my greed and live in paradise for one more day.

The river Stour near Iford

There's a Seal in the river near the Iford bridges,
From the bank, where the Narcissi, are danced upon by swarming clouds of hungry Midges,
A smoker would stand a better chance,
Of preventing their irritating pre-Vampiric dance,
But, if you find a place where you can observe,
Then you will be rewarded in the manner you deserve,
The bridge of rough-hewn sugar lumps of rectangular Purbeck stone,
Makes arches like the rounded back of monsters we have known,
Weary feet, horses hooves, rubber tyres upon that bridge have stood,
That solid bridge has borne them, making no distinction between the evil and the good,
From the bucolic scene at water's edge…look down,
Beyond the water's mirrored surface, above the bed of brown,
Mullet…with their soft and fragile lips…suck the green,
Of the algae formed below the line…they wish to be unseen,
Should you move too quickly or allow your shadow cast,

They disperse in all directions…yes…they disperse…and fast,
For the Mullet know their place in Nature's spinning fortune wheel,
In the river, near Iford bridges…I tell you… there's a Seal.

The view from "Garden end"

If you let your eye run from here… where the garden's ending,
Across the slightly tufty grass… where the lawn is mending,
Past the swaying toad-flax… to the pond,
Containing aqua-characters of whom… we're very fond,
The smart green frog… with brown panels down his sides,
If you see him first, he'll freeze… otherwise he hides,
The newt, who's very slim, resides beneath the silt,
Tapioca frog spawn feast… without a trace of guilt,
Occasionally a toad is found… broader, squat and warty,
He doesn't leap, but he can run… on two back legs… so sporty,
Dragonflies will arise… a finale, exciting but short,
From Nymphs in pond to flying darts… a rise of some import,

Butterflies and Bees... buzz and flutter around the trees,
Buddleia and Lilac... when the sun is felt on my back... in the breeze,
The scent is in the air... yes, over here... no, it's over there,
It moves around the garden, in the way it moves my hair,
The Blue-tit flies from bird-bath, through Wisteria covered arch,
And lands upon the table... for his daily fix of starch,
He pecks a tiny crumb... this little beauty is so small,
Just feathers, beak and tum... and unique song... that's all,
Across the orange gravel to my home,
A brick-built cube to live in... and around it, I can roam,
And keep this piece of heaven from collapsing to the ground,
Whilst keeping nature natural... as long as I'm around...

Dorset Man

There are lizards in the sandy banks, surrounding Shelley Park,
Swings and slides and roundabouts are open... til its dark,
Just half a mile to the south is Boscombe pier and beach,
Where circling seagulls wheel and dive, with wailing mournful screech,
Walk along the platform there, to stand above the sea,
I used to dive from the top, so girls would fancy me,
Below the platform of the pier, with slapping sea and concrete beams,
A different world can be seen, a world of crabs and fish and dreams,
I used to lower a drop-net there, bloody fish-heads used as bait,
Controlling the urge to pull it up... edible crabs for those who wait,
The mighty concrete pillars live a life of dual existence,
A life of wind and sun above...below, cold, dark resistance,
Walk then with feet all bare and carrying your shoes,

Just over a mile to Bournemouth pier and plenty of public loos,
Feel the way that Crusoe did, when his feet dented the sand,
Be grateful then, for all that's offered in this great free promised land,
I'm proud to be a Dorset man. We'll never say we're best,
For in Dorset we are reasonable… and won't disrespect the rest,
That modesty pervades the county and all the folk within,
I'm a British, English, Dorset man and proud of all my kin.

Hip upon the Briar

Coral red…the bead…the hip, where fragrant flower cup,
Had tempted bee and butterfly, to come and land and sup,
The fruit now born, must be borne…once more,
The seeds inside to travel, within their host…as times before,
Passing through the Scrumper…clad in feather or in fur,
Then grows the briar in places…other than it were,
A thorny kingdom…mirror to the other,
Another chance to clamber and to smother,
All…except the strongest of the rivals,
The native cowslips, Dandelions, weeds of ancient survivals,
Lords and ladies…with berries poisonous to us,
Feed the birds with berries…they find sumptuous,
Protected from casual destruction,
By the spikey barb of thorn upon the basket-like construction,
Of the briar,
Coral red, the bead, the hip…Coral red…like fire.

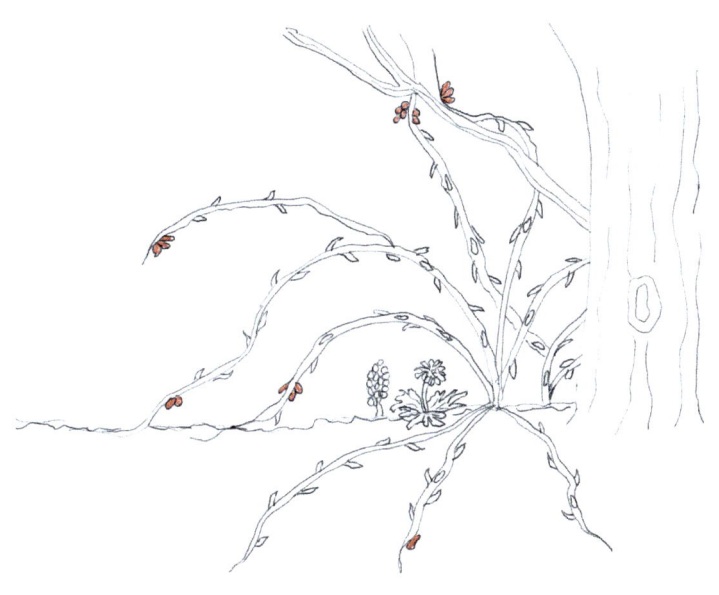

The Oak is dead

The Oak... now dead,
Stands stiff and brittle... like a signpost of the dread,
Its rotting arms pointing, in a gruesome parody,
Of the lightning bolt, that struck this once proud tree,
The Ivy unaffected by what befell its host,
Clings and climbs healthily... round its withered post,
The Ivy's green, makes it look, as though the Oak is growing,
But, one is dead, the other caring little of the going,
Of the life... that left the tree,
When the lightning hit the trunk, with untold energy,
The spark of life has gone,
But the Ivy clambers on...

Dead mouse

Dead mouse in a chestnut husk,
There since dawn? There since dusk?
Lying on the pavement by the trees,
Death by natural causes… old age or disease?
Or did it eat the nut and then the shell?
And quietly choke to death? Pathology could tell,
No post mortem needed for this small soul,
Somewhere quite nearby, waits a silent empty hole.

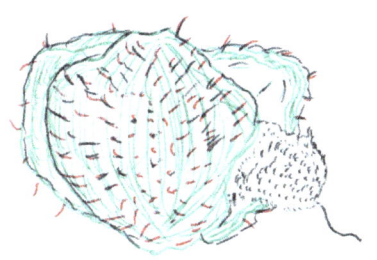

Hedgehog Hotel

My daughters bought my wife a little "hedgehog hotel,"
We placed it down the garden and with leaves we hid it well,
It's like a little igloo… instead of ice…it's made of Wicker,
A little bit like rattan, but stronger and much thicker,
I saw the first guest arrive… a day or two ago,
I tipped my cap, politely saying "Mrs Hedgehog…Hello,"
To my amazement she answered back and this is what she said,
"I'm a Porcine boundary dweller and I'm male… my name is Ted,"
"I'm so very sorry Ted"…I said, my embarrassment spectacular,
"Not to worry chum"…said Ted…"Hedgehog is the vernacular,"
"I'm more upset about your use of gender,"
"But generally to be Human means…to be a repeat offender,"

Ted seemed to be a little on the spikey side,
His little piggy eyes defiant, as he backed indoors to hide,
Muffled from within, I hear him shout…
"Don't you dare put bread and milk down…or I'm moving out!"
A prickly customer…that's what Ted the Porcine boundary dweller is,
But everyone has foibles and Ted just told me his…

Sweet the Robin

Sweet… the Robin and sweet the Robin's song,
His ruddy vest, a welcome flash of colour, when colour has gone,
From all the growing things… which will not flower,
At this particular moment, within cruel winter's hour,
Cheerful… the Robin, or cheerful is how he seems,
To those of us, in winter's grip, who survive with summer's dreams,
Brave… the Robin, brave to get so close to we,
Who span the range of good and bad… with such variety,
He seeks the chaos that we cause, when we to the garden come,
Lifting rocks, pulling weeds… disturbing the equilibrium,
Hungry… the Robin, hungry not for friends,
For unless he gets his share of bugs… That's where his sweet life ends.

The tree by the fence

The squirrel hangs down like a bat,
And feeds upon the sunflower seeds that…
I put into the container to dispense,
Seeds to the birds, from the tree by the fence,
He chews at the opening, to make it bigger,
And he shakes the container, in a bid to trigger,
An avalanche of seeds, to the hole, where he feeds,
Of course he has needs…but I hope he concedes,
Just a little to the birds, who I aimed to entice,
To the tree by the fence…Yes, that would be nice.

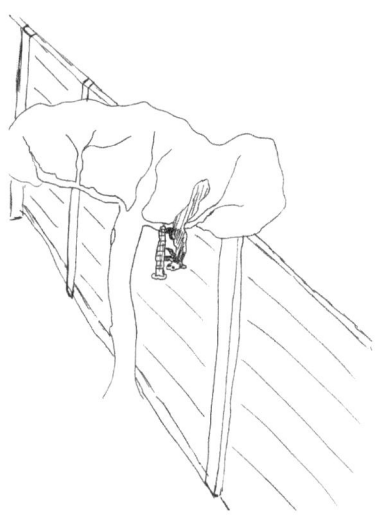

I will be a bird

I will be a bird and I shall sing,
Of all that it took to be a man… everything,
My song will rise and pierce the misty morn,
As I sing of thrilling heart and love's first dawn,

I will be a bird and my music will tell the story,
Of growing strength of body and the promises of glory,
My song will rise and human noise obscure,
As I sing of the importance, that a man is true and sure,

I will be a bird and I will sing for all I'm worth,
Which now… as then… is nothing, but the little piece of earth,
From which I came… and to which, I'll return,
With hope that for the good I've done… a birdsong I will earn.

Index
Poems of general interest

Plan this	82
Turandot (an opera by Giacomo Puccini)	83
Witch's knickers	86
Harry Skinner	88
Scary Cat	89
A miracle of engineering	90
Good men can't hate	92
Time traveller	93
Sharky	94
Lucky	96
Scone	97
A final flight	98
The tribes of Tensular	100
From the Author	112

Plan this (to be read rapidly and exuberantly)

Try to be spontaneous,
Extraneous, sub-cutaneous, more
   right-brain-eous,
Don't be too constructed,
With the vibrancy and immediacy deducted,
Redacted, subtracted,
Just go with the flow,
Don't look for traps, don't wear straps,
Let the time elapse and eventually collapse,
Be spontaneous!

Turandot (based upon an opera by Giacomo Puccini)

Nigh on a score of suitors… to death had been despatched,
When failing to solve three riddles, which Turandot had hatched,
She was a heavenly princess, not of mortal make,
To avenge a forbear's misery, she swore…no man, her heart could take,
Calaf, a prince, of a foreign kingdom born,
Crossed to China from his land, with war and famine torn,
He became entranced, enchanted and attracted,
All other thoughts and cares were… from his mind redacted,
His old blind father, once the king and his servant Liu,
Had searched for many months and entered China too,
They found Calaf… their joy was uncontained,
But, hidden were the bonds, by which the prince was chained,
Refusing to go with them, he insisted on the quest,
Ignoring their wise council… Turandot he'd test,

Three times she set him riddles, deep in cryptic code,
Three times he answered truly and eloquently showed,
His resolve could not be quenched, even by threat of death,
He would fight to win her heart, fight to his last breath,
Turandot was beaten, but hard inside her heart,
And vowed that love's warm embers would never get to start,
So Calaf, bold and confident, offered her a way,
If she discovered what he's called, before the break of day,
Then she could rise once more alone, icy and aloof,
But, if she failed, she must love, with warmth and heat and truth,
Turandot was fury-filled and threatened all will die,
If she has not been told his name, when sunrise lights the sky,
Calaf sings that "none shall sleep," so sure he is of winning,
But, Vinchero is far away, when they drag the old blind king in,

The servant girl steps in front and states, she is the one,
Who knows his name… and to only her, the cruel torture's done,
She won't speak his name, though racked and nearly dead,
Turandot asked her why and this is what Liu said,
"I have always loved the prince… the torture's pain is nought,"
"Against the love, for my beloved, that my silence bought,"
Turandot was beaten, as sweet Liu passed away,
And told Calaf that she was his, it was not yet, the start of day,
The prince… with love requited, revealed that he's Calaf,
Then Turandot, told him of her fear and fire… and wrath,
And though he cannot have her, to heaven she'll now process,
The secret of her fire and passion… will be <u>all</u> he will possess.

'Witch's knickers'

In this age of plastic bags and increased global wind,
It's pretty common to see bags fly and in the branches pinned,
Flying like a windsock, to mark this plastic age,
The poly-flag on flag-pole trees, a wind-direction gauge,

In the 1960's it was similar. The bags were not so many,
There was no charge for small or large, not even one old penny,
But as a boy, in my parent's car, I looked up and I saw them,
I puzzled as to what they were. I could not… ignore them,

I asked my parents to explain. A smile on Mum's face flickers,
She said, "My old Mother told me when young… that they are 'Witch's Knickers',"
"They must have ripped off from the Witch, as by the branch she flew,"
She could not tell me any more…That was all she knew,

And even now… when I walk… and see the knickers flying,
I warn you…don't investigate…to see if they are lying,
The sights I saw…I wish I could forget,
When I googled 'Witch's Knickers'…on the internet.

Harry Skinner

Harry sits, his focus on his fingers, upon the strings,
Of his permanent music-mate, his guitar... and he sings,
The curves of the sound-box, hug above his knee,
And the music that he makes, begs all souls to be free,
The eyes may watch his fingers, trapping notes,
Then releasing with a strum... freed the story floats,
His spirit is somewhere else however...
In the stories that he'll tell forever,
Of friendships and relief,
Of what determines rich or poor, or beggar...or the thief,
Notes that don't need words... fly readily from the hole,
Of Harry Skinner's guitar... the exit from his soul,
There's gravel in his voice... gravel from the trail,
Of every bleeding finger and every broken nail,
Strange it is that pleasure comes, listening to lament,
A cigarette of music pleasure... inhale... until it's spent.

Scary Cat

I once knew a very scary cat,
A grey and white and very hairy cat,
He wore a blue and white hooped woolly hat,
He would sit for hours and smile at me in that,
He was plump and very nearly fat,
He seldom exercised, mainly he was sat,
One day he was there upon the mat,
With a Helium-filled balloon marked... 'Scary Cat.'

A miracle of engineering

In my 1970's automatic stainless Seiko 5,
Is the kind of engineering, which keeps my hopes alive…
Centrally located, in the movement, there's a pin,
Around this pivot point, a demi-lune of steel will spin,
It rotates with the movement of the wrist,
This rotation winds the spring. I hope you get the gist?
The coiled spring stores the power and governs the release,
Enough to turn the cogs and hands, of my humble, old timepiece,
It doesn't need a battery, or the power of the sun,
In fifty years, no service needed, nor a part… not one…
The Swiss (of course) invented, the watch that winds with movement,
The Japanese have made them well, at lower cost…improvement!

A word for Rolex must be spoken, disdain for them's unjust,
As they're a, "Not for profit, international, charitable trust,"
I hope that in the search for power, sun and wind and wave,
That mechanical ingenuity will play its part to save,
The genius of humanity…its bid to grow… survive,
Like the 1970's automatic stainless Seiko 5…

Good men can't hate

Fight not for beauty or indeed for treasure,
Fight for love and only in just measure,
Never in hate is goodness to be found,
Good blood still stains the cold… and foreign ground,
Preserve the wrath for a proven worthy cause,
Give time the chance to heal… and settle not old scores,
When good men see the harm that they've inflicted,
The ire within them… is quickly contradicted,
By the natural mercy cupped in honest heart,
History can be served the best, by the wars that never start.

Time traveller

I once went back in time and saved the world,
The Kings and Queens were grateful and the bunting was unfurled,
By way of thanks, a sealed chest of riches,
Wrapped in purple silk and secured with tiny stiches,
I let them know that I could not return,
I'd used my only wormhole, to solve the world's concern,
It's stable only long enough for me to get back home,
I flicked the switch on my remote…rectangular and chrome,
I heard the royal court's collective gasp,
As I vanished from their vision, the chest was in my grasp,
I appeared at home, as though I'd never left,
I felt the weight of treasure in the box, which had some heft,
I cut the tiny stiches with my knife,
Excited that the contents will really change my life,
Tulip bulbs and two sacks…salt and tea,
That was what the royals thought was apt reward for me,
I plant the tulips in my little garden,
Salt my chips… drink my tea… wait for veins to harden.

Sharky

From Bournemouth to London, then to Miami by Jet,
A week full of meetings and speakers, to forget,
The best thing about being "owned by the Yanks,"
Was their talent for entertaining…for which I say… "Thanks,"
One of the outings, was a boat in the bay,
Fishing for "sail-fish" was the plan for the day,
Miami skyline, impressive to aft,
As the ten-foot swell, raised and lowered our craft,
Being a 'South-coast, proud, English-Brit',
I told the Yank-crew, that I could handle it,
As I stood on the prow…like a royal figure-head,
I had to disguise…that I wished I were dead,
My face was corpse-white…just a hint of the green,
I was swallowing hard lest my biliousness be seen,
The crew were impressed, taken in by my trick,
While all other nations hung their heads and were sick,

Later on and calmer, we all started to fish,
I wanted a fixed spool reel, that was my wish,
I got given a multiplier, the luck of the draw,
"Drop the line to the seabed"…which I had to ignore,
My line had a 'birds-nest'…that's when it gets tangled,
So my bait just kind of hung, under the boat and limply dangled,
My line was soon sorted…upon reeling it in,
Imagine my shock, when I first saw that fin…
A shark, I had hooked and the Yanks rushed to help,
When I shouted SHARK!!!...well more of a yelp,
I reeled in the monster, lowered slowly to deck,
One stone in weight and two feet long…oh bloody heck!
My main concern was the health of the fish,
I insisted quite loudly, that it was my wish,
For the hook to be carefully removed from the mouth,
"Cos that's how we do it in England…the South,"
The Yanks to their credit were practised and good,
And after some photos…like anyone would,
They carefully released it…back to the deep,
The crew named me 'Sharky'…a memory I'll keep.

Lucky

From forming bud to petal's fall,
My roses... I will love them all,
From acorn to oak,
From spark, to fire, to final wisp of smoke,
My love will be my life,
My wife... My dad, my mum, my daughters,
Two full halves... Four full quarters,
Full... Till water brimming over,
Runs down the sides and feeds... the lucky
    clover,
Not as lucky as me,
From seed... a life... then this to see.

Scone

Oh…to spread the jam and dollop cream upon my scone,
Like… bone, cone, hone, phone, stone, tone or zone,
Either way…when I have eaten my sconne,
It's gone…

A final flight

If I lay dying upon my final bed,
I would not waste my precious final thoughts…
   Instead,
I would picture those I love the most… enjoying the delight,
Of a kaleidoscope of butterflies jinking in their flight,
Not leaving, as they have since I was born,
But circling round… just as though… it's to <u>me</u> that they are drawn,
All the colours therein represented,
Their petal wings wafting jasmine, as though those wings are scented,
Like the angels of the flowers,
Their presence alone… enhance my super-powers,
My powers to appreciate the miracle of beauty,
A miracle that many too few… observe… as is our duty,
Reds and yellows, blues and greens… I'm fainting,
My heart cannot contain… the magnificence of this painting,
My final act to smile,
And kiss goodbye my loves… for just a while…

The tribes of 'Tensular'

In a time long-past, for such modern folk as we,
Two tribes lived close together, in moderate harmony,
The townsfolk of 'Tensular', sophisticated for their time,
With halls for music and poets, who made their stories rhyme,
Their leader was a diplomat, skilled in word and action,
'Ursula'… had some control of every dissident faction,
Supported by her Captain, a soldier from wars before,
'Regulat'…efficient at… keeping violence from her door,
Don't misunderstand the picture, that I paint,
All is fair and reasonable…there's freedom and restraint,
It's a democratic town and with a democratic vote,
'Ursula' is trusted, to keep all things afloat,
'Regulat' has an army of roughly company strength,
They all have other jobs, which I won't explain at length,
But, a blacksmith called 'Clang' and a carpenter named 'Splinter',

Had been hardened to a lethal point, by training through the winter,
The town had some defences, as you might expect,
Sharpened trunk…angled…sunk, with moat below…protect,
One thousand 'Tensulayans', who live within this ring,
At the foot of 'Tensul Mountain'… moat fed by 'Tensul spring',
The mountain people live, in a different way to this,
Rugged and related… cousins often kiss,
Again… please don't misconstrue, my few words to describe,
These hardy 'Tensul-mountain folk'… are a worthy noble tribe,
Their leader takes the name of a fearless mountain cat,
His name is 'Puma', black hair and beard, tied useful in a plait,
He's a leader based on merit… like 'Ursula' in town,
No 'Regulat' however, to put the bad boys down,
This is work he does himself and does it very well,
Though wise and kind, he's capable of blows of deathly fell,

His hunting prowess, is only matched, by one within his clan,
His son... is why he stays as chief...a promising young man,
The son is known as 'Tento-bar' and he's in love already,
With the fierce and beauteous 'Shinka'... yes in love and going steady.
One morning from the summit hut, 'Shinka' looked due east,
And what she saw, was the sight... 'Tensulayans' like the least,
The blood-red sails of the pitch black boats,
As the raiding 'Golcan' pillagers... bring death upon their floats,
This time there were many... invasion was their plan,
'Shinka' ran down the rocky slope, to warn her beloved man,
'Tento-bar', on being told, blew his mighty horn,
A blast so full of power, the note carried on the dawn,
All the way to 'Tensular'... 'Clang' put down his hammer,
"What the f-f-f- heck was that"? Asked 'Splinter' with a stammer,
'Clang' smiled..."The horn of 'Tento-bar'... granting us a warning,"

"Fetch your deadly bow, my friend… we fight to live this morning."

'Regulat' was busy barking orders at his fighters,
Shouting at the gatemen and the specialist fire-lighters,
To ignite the beacons that they'll use, to flame the tips of arrows,
To send a hail of fire, as their foe comes through the narrows,
'Ursula' asked 'Regulat'…"Are we in real danger?"
He smiled at her with confidence… "You treat me like a stranger?"
"I have twelve score of 'Tensulayans' trained and armed and ready,"
"I suggest you show composure and your nerve is seen as steady,"
'Ursula' was a little shocked at 'Regulat's' demeanour,
She had rarely known him patronise and never seen him keener,
"Thank you 'Regulat'," she said, her diplomatic skills,
She would have to use in dealing… with a man, who loves his kills.

'Splinter' was an archer, his bow, the finest yew,
He had made all the bows, but he kept the one most true,
'Angel' he had named it, after a girl that he adored,
It also had the duty… of sending souls up to the lord,
He stood on the platform, behind the sharpened logs,
Above the moat… the archers, so they could see the dogs,
The dogs that are the 'Golcans', men who raid and kill,
Hungry for, what is not theirs… they won't stop until…
All are dead and Ursula's head is hoisted on a spear,
"Well that ain't going to happen, not while me and 'Clang' are here,"
'Clang' was at the head of the two ranks by the gate,
He made all the swords and his own… he endowed with mighty weight,
'Clang' was a behemoth at fully seven feet,
When not engaged in warfare, his temperament was sweet,
Rending iron had made him muscular, but in his heart you'd find,

A man of consideration, of loyalty… and genuinely kind,
This day he would stand… and blows he would deliver,
Like a mighty oak fighting off, the swollen raging river,
"I will live to see the snow on 'Tensul-top' this winter,"
"We can fight off anyone…me and my mate 'Splinter',"
'Skagg' jumped off the boat, two-footed and landed clean,
His tattoos depicted murders and the action he had seen,
The chief of the 'Golcans' and heartless to his core,
His addiction fed at every turn… to blood and power and war,
Jumping up upon a rock, he counted the ships that were landing,
His army of one thousand men… were hungry, angry, standing…
Waiting for the order to march on 'Tensul town',
'Tensular'…where women are…"Let's bring their men-folk down,"
'Skagg' had inside knowledge, of the numbers that defend,
He had been told, by a traitor bold, that victory would depend,

Upon having greater numbers than, the two hundred and forty men,
Who stand in 'Tensular' this day, just across that fen,
'Regulat' had been busy… it was he who sent that note,
From his room, war he'd groomed and from it I will quote…
"I will give you many women and plenty precious metals,"
"All I ask in return, is when the war-dust settles,"
"That I be king of 'Tensular'… and its mountain tall,"
"By my side, will be 'Ursula', a slave in her own hall,"
A bitter man he had become, his ego bloated… large,
Resenting orders from a woman…He should be in charge,
And so, he plotted against his own, his soldiers and his kin,
He would load the dice for 'Skagg'… and help the 'Golcans' win.

On the mountain, the little camp of forty mountain folk,
Packed their weapons…spears and knives and donned their travel cloak,

'Puma', 'Tento-bar', thirty men, seven women and 'Shinka',
Had talked of how they would assist…'Puma' was a thinker,
They would wait camouflaged, until the battle started,
Then they'd kill them from the rear…hunt them dead…cold-hearted,
Sharp-eyed 'Shinka' saw the 'Golcans', marching on the town,
In single file, the mountain hunters… took the thin path down.

Arrows lit… 'Splinter' waited, for the foe to be sighted,
The 'Golcans' sped the narrow path …Whoosh… the arrows flaming, flighted…
Hit their mark…'Golcans' fell, ten or twenty, who could tell,
Jumping over former friends…burning bodies… flaming hell,
Three more times…flying sticks of piercing fire,
Lit the night, the path a choking, burning funeral pyre,
Nine hundred 'Golgans' hit the gate,
A furious mass of flailing iron and full of burning hate,
'Clang', his massive arms, like pistons cleaving,
Slashing, flashing blade, honed to sharpness… leaving,

Bodies at every point of contact…wounded or cut dead,
Furious…breathless…animals…none will keep their head,

As the battle raged at the entrance to the town,
The forty 'Tensul-mountain', hunter-killers had come down,
And quietly come up, behind their quarry, bringing up the rear,
Forty 'Golcan' throats were cut, from ear to filthy ear,
Six hundred 'Golcan' soldiers, forced their way, into the town,
So far four hundred had been killed, or at least, wounded down,
But 'Skagg' was still confident, his enemies would eat dirt,
Showing all his grisly tattoos, neath his rent and tattered shirt,
One tattoo in particular, his character to attest,
A black and shrivelled heart tattoo, on the left side of his chest,
It was now that he called upon, 'Regulat' his clown,
With fifty of his loyal men, not loyal to the town,
They turned and joined the 'Golcan', with promises of power,
This shift in numbers, seems to be, the decider of the hour,

'Clang' and 'Splinter' and fifty men, are gathered in a ring,
'Ursula' in the centre starts to calm and strongly sing,
The song all 'Tensulayans' know, the soaring notes imbue,
The people who belong to it… to do or die…they do…
'Puma', 'Tento-bar' and 'Shinka' are also in this group,
Forty 'Tensulayans' and ten of the mountain troop,
'Skagg' and three hundred 'Golcans' and 'Regulat' of course,
Shout down, the stirring singing and in a voice…battle hoarse,
'Skagg' says to Ursula…"Your head, you will not lose,"
"Regulat has plans for you…in a way you would not choose",
'Ursula' just smiled, put two fingers to her lips,
And whistled such a piercing note, then put her hands on hips,
As ten-score 'Tensul' women, filed from the main town hall,
Led by 'Angel'…'Splinter's' love…they were archers…all,
'Ursula', had feared that 'Regulat' had designs,
Upon taking over 'Tensul town', yes…she'd read the signs,

She had two hundred secret bows, made by trusted 'Splinter',
In the town hall, he'd taught them well, at night time in the winter,
'Angel' took an arrow, with steady hand, from her quiver,
Aimed it at 'Skagg's' heart tattoo, quickly to deliver,
A fatal piercing, the last that he would know,
Was the yew-wood arrow, passing through from 'Angel's' lovely bow,
A cheer went up and 'Clang' stepped forth,
'Regulat' stared in dread,
'Clang's' mighty blade scythed the air and parted the traitor's head,
From his body… which then fell and bled upon 'Tensul' earth,
Two hundred arrows met their mark. Two hundred cursed their birth,
One hundred 'Golcans' ran away, back to boat and sea,
No more invasions by that tribe…no more iniquity.
'Puma' married 'Ursula'… how could he resist?
A woman with a clever mind and he her iron fist,
'Tento-bar' and 'Shinka' became the leaders on the mountain,

They were married in that year, in town near 'Tensul' fountain,
'Clang' had built the fountain so both the tribes remember,
How they had come together, that terrible November,
'Splinter' and his 'Angel', got married there as well,
Much beer was drunk, so they say…so the stories tell,
Many men were buried…many children needed now,
'Clang' has sired so many… his giant seed he'd plough,
So now, it's said of 'Tensular' their men are strong and tall,
Their women famed for archery. That town will never fall…

From the Author

As if I haven't talked too much already!

Thank you for buying this 2nd book in the Poeticus Pictoralis series.

I write at least one poem a week to take to my Mum (88) and see how her painting is coming on, that's if she's not too busy gardening or achieving a DIY project.

Her impressionist seascapes are the covers of the books and also some of the paintings within.

I am also lucky to be married to Angie and the father of Jane & Vic and because we have made each other's birthday cards for a number of years… I have even more water colours and pen & pencil drawings and digital art to choose from.

I have included some of my scribbles… I'm not an artist, but I left them in because there is something to be said for expression, even in the absence of talent.

The first book sold very well for a self-published book of poetry from a "non-famous" person.

I would like to thank all the people who have purchased a copy themselves and/or who have encouraged others to do so.

It is not a profitable venture, but, my motives are… to please my mum and leave a verbal and visual legacy for my children and anyone who is interested.

Thank you again.
With Love,
Crispin

Lightning Source UK Ltd.
Milton Keynes UK
UKHW050201200522
403133UK00006B/9